NATURE WATCH

HIPPOS

Revised Edition

Written by
Sally M. Walker

Lerner Publications Company • Minneapolis

Special thanks to Dr. William Barklow of the Biology Department of Framingham College in Massachusetts for sharing his vast knowledge of hippos.

Text copyright © 2008 by Sally M. Walker

Lerner Publications Company
A division of Lerner Publishing Group, Inc.
241 First Avenue North
Minneapolis, MN 55401 U.S.A.

Website address: www.lernerbooks.com

Library of Congress Cataloging-in-Publication Data

Walker, Sally M.
    Hippos / by Sally M. Walker. — Rev. ed.
        p.   cm. – (Nature watch)
    Includes bibliographical references and index.
    ISBN-13: 978–0–8225–7512–2 (lib. bdg. : alk. paper)
    1. Hippopotamus—Juvenile literature. 2. Pygmy
hippopotamus—Juvenile literature. I. Title.
QL737.U57W34 2008
599.63'5—dc22   2007013576

Manufactured in the United States of America
1 2 3 4 5 6 – DP – 13 12 11 10 09 08

CONTENTS

Above: A large group of hippos enjoys the water at Serengeti National Park in Tanzania.
Right: This hippo's eyes and ears just barely peek out of the water.

INTRODUCTION

LIKE A MIRROR, THE CALM SURFACE OF A LAKE IN AFRICA reflects the blue sky and fluffy white clouds. Slowly, two goggly eyes ease out of the water. Next, two nostrils blow a spray of water into the air. Gradually, a gigantic head appears. An enormous mouth yawns so wide that you could almost climb inside and sit. Of course, you wouldn't. The long tusks and sharp front teeth send a very clear message. This watering hole is for hippopotamuses, not you!

   The hippopotamus is the third-largest land mammal in the world. Only the elephant and the rhinoceros are bigger. Because the name hippopotamus is long, most people call it hippo for short. For a long time,

The name *hippopotamus* comes from two Greek words—*hippos* and *pota-mos*. Together, they mean "river horse." This name might make you think these animals are related to horses, but they are not.

Scientists once thought that hippos were closely related to pigs. But later studies said a hippo's closest relative may be a dolphin (*left*) or a whale.

scientists believed that hippos were related to pigs. But new studies of hippos suggest that their closest relatives may be dolphins and whales!

FOSSIL FINDS

Scientists try to figure how long hippo **species**, or kinds, have existed. They look at the **fossil** record. Fossils are traces or remains of animals or plants that, over thousands of years, have slowly turned into stone. The fossil record is a collection of all the information on each species that scientists have gathered from fossils around the world.

Tracing a family tree through the fossil record is not always easy. Imagine the record as pieces of a large puzzle that have been scattered around your home for months. Like the puzzle in your home, pieces of the fossil record are frequently missing. So scientists have a hard time telling exactly when a species first existed. But based on fossil evidence, scientists believe that the anthracotheres, a group of mammals that lived between 25 and 40 million years ago, are the immediate ancestors of modern hippos.

From 10,000 to 40,000 years ago, many species of hippos roamed throughout Asia, Africa, and central Europe. Although hippos were common and widespread then, only two species are still alive. They are the common hippo and the pygmy hippo. Both species are found only in Africa, south of the Sahara. And both species are struggling to survive.

WHERE HIPPOS LIVE

The common hippo (*Hippopotamus amphibius*) spends much of its time in shallow rivers and lakes in eastern and southern Africa. These waters form their main **habitat**, or living space. However, some common hippos don't mind the

The Democratic Republic of the Congo (DRC, once called Zaire) had a hippo population of 30,000 in 1994. Since then, political struggles have changed the country. Scientists think the DRC's hippo population is down by 95 percent. This means only about 1,500 common hippos still live there.

Common hippos cool off in a river in Africa. This kind of hippo loves the water—and company.

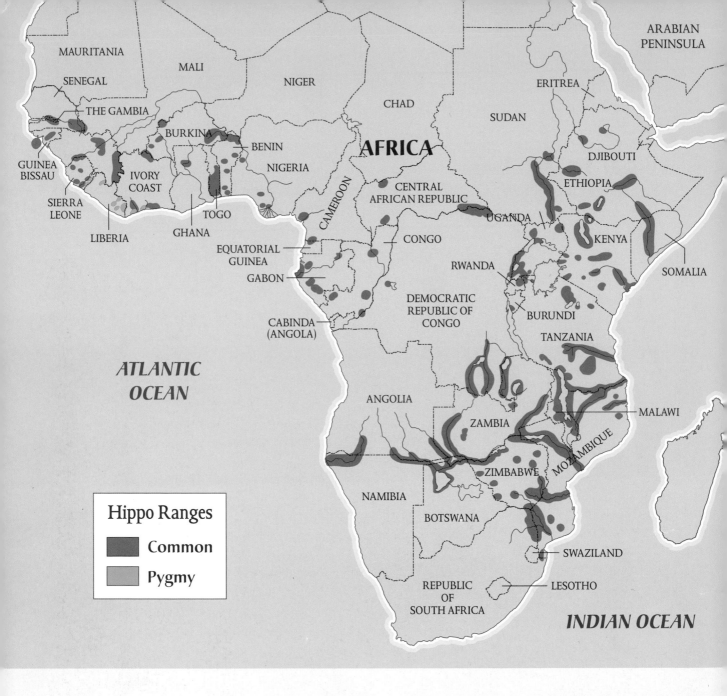

salty water of ocean lagoons in other parts of Africa. Between 125,000 and 155,000 of these huge hippos are left in the wild. Most live in open areas of Uganda, Kenya, Tanzania, Zambia, and Mozambique.

The pygmy hippo (*Hexaprotodon liberiensis*) is found mostly in Liberia. A few live in Sierra Leone and the Ivory Coast. Some scientists think a few still inhabit Guinea, Guinea-Bissau, and Nigeria. Other scientists are not so sure. All of these countries are in western Africa.

Unlike common hippos, pygmy hippos prefer a forested habitat. These shy creatures spend their days hidden in rivers and swamps that are overhung with shrubs and trees. With increasing speed, people are clearing these forests to make room for farms. For this reason, pygmy hippos are in far more danger of **extinction** (the death of all members of the species) than common hippos are.

The exact number of pygmy hippos isn't known. But zoologists (scientists who study animal life) estimate that probably only 2,000 still live in the wild. Another 350 live in zoos around the world. Pygmy hippos are hard to locate in the wild. Most of what we know about them has been learned by studying hippos in zoos.

This pygmy hippo grazes near a forest in the Ivory Coast.

GETTING WORSE

In the mid-1990s, the International Union for the Conservation of Nature and Natural Resources (IUCN) made studies of the two hippo species. The group wanted to find out the size of hippo populations. From the studies, scientists listed the common hippo as of least concern. This meant they were at low risk of becoming extinct. They ranked the pygmy hippo as **vulnerable**. This meant that, unless changes took place, the animal might become extinct.

In 2004, however, the IUCN made another study. Scientists had seen big habitat losses for both species. They were worried about the populations. These scientists recommended that common hippos be listed as vulnerable. They put pygmy hippos in the **endangered** category. This meant the animal is at high risk of becoming extinct. In 2006, the IUCN made these changes official.

PHYSICAL TRAITS

EVEN THOUGH ONLY TWO SPECIES EXIST, THE MEMBERS don't look very much alike. At a quick glance, you might think that size is the only difference between common and pygmy hippos. But they also differ in shape and in the location of their eyes and nostrils.

BODY SIZES AND SHAPES

Common hippos are much larger than pygmy hippos. The males of both species, called **bulls**, are larger than the females, or **cows**. Common hippo bulls are about 4.5 to 5.5 feet (1.4–1.7 m) tall at the shoulder and are about 11.5 feet (3.5 m) long. They weigh between 3,500 and 7,000 pounds (1,589–3,178 kg). Some very large common hippo bulls can reach 8,000 pounds (3,632 kg). In height and length, common hippo cows are several inches shorter than bulls. They generally weigh between

1,500 and 5,100 pounds (681–2,315 kg).

Compared to common hippos, pygmy hippos seem tiny. They measure 30 to 39 inches (76–99 cm) tall at the shoulder. On average, they are 5 feet (1.5 m) in length. Pygmies seldom weigh more than 500 pounds (227 kg). This is about the same size as a large hog.

The common hippo has a barrel-shaped body and short, stocky legs. The short legs do not raise its body very far off the ground. Often its belly scrapes along the ground as it moves. The animal leaves behind a shallow trench between its right and left footprints.

The common hippo also has a very large, heavy head *(left)*. It can make up almost one-third of a hippo's length and

The common hippo has short, stocky legs in comparison to its large, rounded body.

weigh almost 1,000 pounds (454 kg). That's about as heavy as a dozen fifth graders. The muscles in a hippo's short, thick neck have to be very strong to support its heavy head.

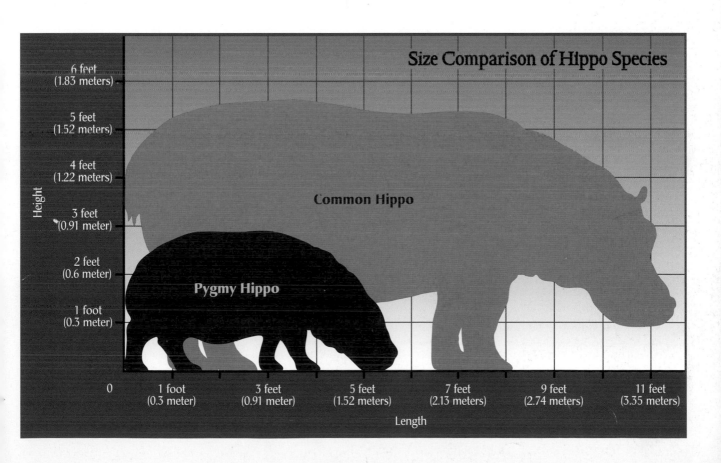

Top: **The pygmy hippo has a more slender body than the common hippo and is almost black in color.**
Bottom: **The common hippo can be brownish gray, like this one, or more of a grayish purple.**

In contrast, the pygmy hippo's body is more long and slender. The animal is shaped more like a torpedo than a barrel. Its legs are much slimmer and longer in relation to its body size. A pygmy hippo's head is smaller. Its neck is less chunky.

HIPPO SKIN

Both hippo species have thick, wrinkly skin. These features are also common to a group of animals called pachyderms. Elephants and rhinoceroses belong to this group as well.

The skin in some areas of the hippo's body—such as the chest and neck—is particularly thick. These areas are important targets for **predators** such as hyenas, lions, and crocodiles. They kill and eat calves and sick adult hippos. The common hippo's skin may be as thick as 2 inches (5 cm) in these exposed areas. Hippos have rolls of skin around their necks and near the tops of their legs. A layer of fat lies beneath the skin in both species.

Pachyderm comes from two Greek words, *pachys* and *derma*, which mean "thick skin."

Common hippos may appear grayish brown or grayish purple on top. Their bellies are usually pink. Pygmy hippos are almost black on top, sometimes with a greenish tinge. Their bellies are grayish yellow or cream colored.

Years ago, people believed that hippos could sweat blood. Hippos have glands (body organs) under their skin that produce a salty, oily, reddish brown liquid. In some light, this liquid looks a little bit like blood. The liquid seeps out of the hippo's skin to keep it moist and protected from the hot sun. The red liquid may also kill germs and help skin wounds heal.

This close-up view of a hippo shows its thick, wrinkled skin. This hippo also has the reddish brown liquid on his skin that protects the hippo from the sun.

Hippos have stretchy skin connecting their toes. This webbing helps them swim more easily.

FEET AND TOES

With their large body size, common hippos need strong legs and firm footing. Each of a hippo's large, rounded feet has four toes. This is a feature of a group of hoofed mammals called even-toed ungulates. Camels, giraffes, deer, and pigs are also members of this group.

Unlike the feet of these other even-toed ungulates, hippo toes are connected by stretchy skin, giving them a webbed look. Webbed feet help a hippo push through water more easily than it could if the toes were not connected.

A pygmy hippo's toes have less webbing. This is probably because it spends more time on land.

When a hippo takes a step, its toes spread out flat on the ground. Each one receives a share of the animal's weight. A pygmy hippo's toes spread out more than a common hippo's do. This gives it better balance as it moves over uneven, forest-covered ground. In both species, a pad on the bottom of each foot acts like a cushion. The cushion softens the weight of heavy hippo footsteps.

In spite of their clumsy-looking bodies, hippos can spin around fast. They can climb steep riverbanks. If they need to, they can even gallop at speeds up to 30 miles per hour (48 km/h) for short distances. For longer distances, they go with a choppy, ground-covering trot. When hippos meet obstacles, they don't jump over them. They either push them aside or go around them.

EYES, EARS, AND NOSTRILS

The placement of a hippo's eyes and nostrils also differ between the two species. On a common hippo's head, the ears, eyes, and nostrils are level with one another, along the top of the head. This way, a common hippo resting under the water needs to rise up only a little ways to be able to hear, see, and breathe.

A pygmy hippo's eyes are located more on the sides of the head. This location helps the hippo see both ahead and to the side as it wanders through the forest. Its nostrils are positioned lower on its muzzle than a common hippo's. This is probably because it does not spend as much time underwater.

Above: The pygmy hippo's eyes and ears are located on the sides of its head. Pygmy hippos spend more time searching for food in the forest. They need to see to the front and sides.
Right: Common hippos have eyes and ears on the top of their heads. When they raise their heads from the water, eyes, ears, and nostrils appear at once.

Top: **This common hippo's ears and nostrils are tightly closed under the water.**
Bottom: **All hippos blow water out of their nostrils when they surface from a lake or river.**

Still, both species stay in the water to escape the African heat. When they dive, they fold their ears against their heads. At the same time, both the common hippo's narrow nostrils and the pygmy hippo's rounder ones close tightly. The nostrils remain closed as long as the hippo is underwater. Full-grown adults can stay under for about five minutes. But a **calf** (baby hippo) can only manage about 20 seconds. When hippos surface, they snort to blow water away from their nostrils. They shake their ears to dry them.

Biologists don't think it is likely that hippos have sharp eyesight. Even if they had good vision, they wouldn't be able to see much. The murky water they live in limits how far they can see. But at night, hippos can see in the dark well enough to wander on land looking for food.

EATING HABITS

Hippos are **herbivores**. These animals eat only plants. Most of the common hippo's 42 to 44 teeth and the pygmy hippo's 38 teeth are used for chewing. Hippos also have 28 **premolars** and **molars**. These are the wide, ridged teeth on the sides and in the back of its mouth. These teeth mash and grind up food before it is swallowed.

The hippo's **incisors** (sharp front teeth) and **canine teeth** (tusks) are used only for protection. These teeth grow throughout a hippo's life. Molars, however, do not keep growing. To help them last, molars have a hard covering called enamel. (Human teeth do too.) But constant grinding does wear down teeth. If the molars become too worn, a hippo can't eat, and it will starve.

After a hippo swallows, the food travels down to its stomach. There, the nutrients from the food are digested (broken down and absorbed into the body). Whatever is left is passed out as **feces**, or solid waste (poop). A hippo's diet contains a lot of cellulose. This material makes up the woody parts of plants. The large amount of cellulose remaining after digestion causes hippos to make lots of solid waste.

Hippos have premolars and molars to chew the plants that make up their diet. They also have incisors and canine teeth in front to use for protection

The hippos' solid waste has a purpose in nature. It helps important nutrients (foods) grow in river habitats. The nutrients are eaten by tiny life-forms. These small creatures are then eaten by bigger life-forms, including fish, reptiles, and birds.

COMMUNICATION

WHETHER FEEDING ON LAND OR RESTING IN THE WATER, hippos use a number of sounds to communicate. They range widely from high-pitched squeaks to deep bass notes. Biologist Dr. William Barklow and other biologists have spent years recording the sounds made by common hippos.

SOUND STUDIES

Using special underwater microphones, the biologists heard sounds similar to the clicks that dolphins and whales make. (As far as biologists know, hippo clicks are used only to communicate. Dolphins and whales use them to pinpoint location.) The biologists also heard fluttery sounds. These noises reminded them of the sounds people can make if they stick out their tongues and blow.

The scientists also heard loud underwater bellows. These sounds were loud enough to make them cover their ears. As the scientists recorded these sounds, they realized something very interesting. People on the riverbank couldn't hear some of the loudest underwater bellows. Yet other sounds recorded below the surface were heard on land. How do hippos do that?

Sound waves in the air can't travel into water. They bounce off the water's surface. And sound waves in water don't travel up into the air. Therefore, the researchers knew that sounds heard in both places had to come from two places in the common hippo's body.

One place was above the water's surface. Out-of-the-water sounds are made two ways. They can be hummed through either the hippo's nostrils or through its mouth. The other place was below the water. Underwater sounds start in the hippo's **larynx**, or voice box. They travel through the fatty roll of skin and muscle on the hippo's throat and pass into the water. With these options, bathing hippos can communicate beneath the water without making a sound above the surface (*left*). Or they can broadcast to both places at once.

Common hippos (here napping in the mud) can communicate through sounds when they are on land or in the water.

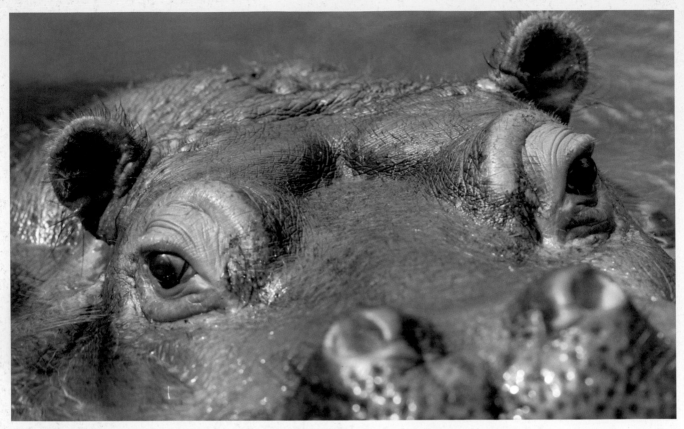

Hippos use their ears when listening out of the water. But under the water, sound passes through their jaws to their inner ears.

Hippos have a special way of hearing underwater sounds. The sounds pass through a hippo's jaws. Then they go directly into its inner ears, where sound is sensed. Hippos can tell a sound's location by comparing the sound levels absorbed by their right and left jaws. If the sound from the left side is louder, they know the sound came from the left. In cloudy rivers, determining a sound's location can be helpful to hippos.

EXPERIMENT HERE
Humans hear poorly underwater. Hippos hear well and can pinpoint location. To hear the difference, try this experiment. Close your eyes and duck underwater. Have a friend click two stones together beneath the surface. You'll find you can hear the sound, but you can't tell which direction it came from. In water, our human ears stop us from pinpointing the source of the sound.

MARKING
TERRITORY

RECOGNIZING SOUNDS AND THEIR SOURCES KEEPS A common hippo bull aware of who is close by. This is particularly important at mating time. He may be able to find bulls that may be wandering into his mating territory.

Bulls stake their territories along riverbanks *(above)*. The **dominant**, or strongest, bulls set up their territories in the nicest places. These spots are in easy reach of water and are close to females. Younger, weaker bulls make their territories farther away. A younger bull must fight and defeat an older bull to win a better territory. Females seldom fight, unless they are protecting their young. But when it is necessary, they are tough fighters. Bulls of both species will fight viciously to protect their mating territories from intruders. But unless a bull is challenged for his territory, he doesn't usually start fights.

In fact, the way a bull marks his territory sends a very clear message to would-be intruders. He rapidly switches his tail as he produces solid waste. The flipping action scatters the solid waste (and the bull's smell) for several yards around. This action makes the statement, "Someone lives here!" Females rarely perform this kind of territorial marking. They don't mind when other hippos cross their paths.

Flying feces makes hippo areas rather messy. But hippos don't mind the mess at all. However, zookeepers find it very hard to keep hippo pens clean.

BULL FIGHTS

Dominant bulls usually tolerate other bulls in their territories as long as the intruders acknowledge who is boss. Hippo fights, which most often take place in or near the water, can last up to several hours. They are very bloody. So when a bull strays into another bull's territory, he is first given a warning. The dominant bull makes a wide yawn that shows off his sharp canine teeth.

The two bulls keep yawning at each other, each time more widely. They may

Hippo bulls mark their territory by flipping their tale and scattering their feces around the area.

Hippo bulls will sometimes scoop water into their mouths and throw it at one another as they fight.

also lunge at each other. But unless the intruder intends to challenge for territory, he backs down and retreats. If the intruder refuses to retreat, the two bulls may scoop up water in their mouths and toss it at each other. Then the two bulls run headlong at each other, mouths open wide. Growling, honking, roaring, and snorting noises are also part of the fight.

A bull may hold the same territory for a few months. If the area is not disturbed by drought or people, he may have it for several years. One bull in Uganda defended the same territory for more than 12 years.

Bulls' canine teeth are valuable weapons for slashing at one another's front legs. A common hippo's canines often grow as long as 20 inches (51 cm). The largest modern hippo canine tooth recorded is 25.5 inches (65 cm). These tusks can cause real problems for a victim.

Standing head to tail, the two bulls continue to bite and batter each other until one of them surrenders, retreats, or is killed. Male hippos get many deep wounds during a fight. The skin of older hippos is often crisscrossed with scars. Sometimes one of the fighters ends up bleeding to death. If a bull is wounded so badly that he is unable to stand, he will likely starve.

Common hippo bull fights are violent. Often one of the bulls dies as a result of his injuries.

MAKING
BABY HIPPOS

THE BULL WITH THE BEST TERRITORY ALSO HAS THE MOST chances for mating, because cows don't look far for a mate. Cows of both species are usually about 3 to 4 years of age when they first come into **estrus**, the time when they can become pregnant. However, they often don't breed until they are several years older. Males are able to breed by the time they are about 5 years old. But because they must compete against dominant bulls, most males don't mate until they are a few years older.

FINDING A MATE AND MATING
Common hippo cows in the wild usually come into estrus at the end of the two dry seasons, in February and August. There is a very good reason for this timing. About 8 months after the calves are born *(above),*

one of the two rainy seasons will be in full swing. At these times of year, ample food is available for cows and their calves.

Biologists don't know how a cow chooses the bull she mates with. But a common hippo cow in estrus often makes a huffing sound, which attracts the attention of nearby bulls. No one has witnessed pygmy hippos mating in the wild. But among pygmy hippos in zoos, a cow does not do anything to get a bull's attention. He seems to know when she is in estrus. He remains close by and sometimes smacks his lips.

Mating itself occurs in shallow water. The cow may move away from the bull three or four times before she lets him mount her. After mating, the cow and bull don't stay together. The next time the cow is in estrus, she may choose either the same bull or a different one. Cows seem to prefer to mate with dominant bulls, rejecting younger or less dominant bulls.

CALF DEVELOPMENT

The calf grows inside its mother for about 7 to 8 months. Just before giving

In 2007, the Louisville Zoo in Louisville, Kentucky, celebrated the birth of a pygmy hippo. The zookeepers set up a contest to name the new calf. They got more than two thousand suggestions. Five-year-old Aspen Hoffmans won the contest. Her name-winning entry was Isoke. This word means "satisfying gift" in the eastern African language of Swahili.

Left: Isoke, a baby pygmy hippo, has her picture taken with her mom, Tracy, at the Louisville Zoo in Kentucky in 2007.

This pygmy hippo calf nurses from its mother. Hippo calves can also nurse while underwater.

birth, the cow becomes restless. She moves to a private place where she can give birth alone.

Common hippos are born in the water. The calf seems to know instinctively (without being taught) how to get to the surface for its first breath of air. Pygmy hippo calves don't instinctively head for the surface. They sometimes drown when they are born in the water. For that reason, zookeepers keep pygmy hippo cows out of water when they are ready to give birth.

Newborn calves seem tiny when compared to their mothers. Common calves range from 50 to 100 pounds (23–45 kg) and are about 3 feet long (0.9 m) and 1.5 feet tall (0.5 m). Pygmy calves weigh 6 to 14 pounds (2.7–6.4 kg) and are about 1

foot (0.3 m) long. Within several minutes of birth, calves of both species are able to walk.

Shortly after birth, the calf nuzzles around its mother's body until it finds one of her two nipples and begins to nurse (feed on the mother's milk). Something very interesting happens when common hippo calves nurse. While they are sucking, their ears fold against their heads and their nostrils close tightly. These actions are the same for when they dive underwater. But the calves do this even when they are nursing on land. They must have to stop breathing to nurse. Since calves often nurse underwater, closing the ears and nose keeps water from getting in and causing harm.

Hippo babies stick close to their mothers both on land *(above)* and in the water *(right)*, like these common hippo calves.

In common hippo calves, this closing of the ears and nose happens on its own. It's not something they must learn. Pygmy calves, however, must learn this trick. Until they do, they nurse on land. All calves frequently nurse underwater. They pop to the surface every few seconds to breathe.

At about 4 months old, calves begin to add plants to their diet. By about 8 months, they eat only solid food. During these early months, calves gain weight fast. A common hippo calf packs on about 10 pounds (4.5 kg) per day. Pygmy calves gain about 1 pound (0.5 kg) per day.

NURSERY SCHOOL

For the first few weeks after birth, a common hippo calf and its mother remain alone. (Pygmy hippos are almost always on their own.) Eventually, common hippos return to the **herd**, or group of hippos to which they belong.

After rejoining the herd, the common hippo cow and calf become members of a **crèche**, a kind of hippo nursery school. The crèche is located in an area close to water, where hippos feel safe. There, calves play with other hippos their age. The females often play hide-and-seek games. The males tend to fight fake battles. All baby hippos like to roll around in the water.

Cows share the job of babysitting for the crèche's young. Taking turns, one or two mothers stay near the calves and keep a lookout for predators. Meanwhile, the other mothers are free to leave the crèche.

In addition to guarding against predators, the babysitters watch out for wandering bulls that might accidentally crush a calf. A bull in a mean mood might even attack a baby hippo. A quiet bull who behaves himself properly may be allowed into the crèche. But if he becomes rowdy, the cows will chase him away.

This common hippo mother and calf have joined a herd of other female hippos and their babies.

Mom Is in Charge

Hippo mothers are very protective of their babies. They are also strict about how they expect a calf to behave. When outside of the crèche, common hippo calves stay close to their mothers. They often climb up on their mothers' backs. If danger threatens, a cow can easily protect her calf by placing her body between it and a predator.

At times, a cow may have several of her calves living with her. (Female calves often remain with their mothers as long as 4 years. A male calf may leave when he is as young as 1 year.) On the way to grazing areas, calves form a line behind their mother according to age. The youngest calf walks closest to the cow. The oldest takes up the rear.

A cow that is angry with her calf is not shy about letting the youngster know it. When a calf doesn't pay attention or refuses to obey, its mother nudges it with her head. Continued misbehavior earns a harsh nip. In severe cases, the mother bonks the calf with her head, sometimes hard enough to knock the baby off its feet.

This common hippo cow gives a warning as a bull comes near her calf.

Top: A mother and baby pygmy hippo take a nap together in the mud. Hippo calves don't stray very far from their mother.
Bottom: Hippo cows nudge their calves with their heads to make sure they behave.

Cows and calves show their affection for one another by nuzzling and licking. They also lightly scrape one another's skin with their canine teeth. This feels good to them in much the same way a back scratch feels good to humans.

Healthy cows are able to give birth every 2 to 3 years until they reach old age. Both species of hippo can live about 30 to 35 years in the wild. But human hunters make that life span hard to reach.

Hippos in zoos often live longer than the normal hippo life span of 30 years or so. The zoos' medical care, healthy food, and safe environment all contribute to long life. The oldest hippo on record died at the age of 61 in a German zoo.

This common hippo calf nuzzles her mother at a safari park in Great Britain.

DAILY ROUTINE

ADULT PYGMY HIPPOS PREFER TO REMAIN ALONE. THEY don't form herds. A cow and her calf will stay together. But pygmy bulls don't like to be in groups. In zoos, pygmy hippos become angry if they are forced to be too close to one another. In contrast, common hippos don't seem to mind one another's company. Their herds usually have between five and one hundred members.

SLEEP TIME
Common hippo herds rest most of the time *(above)*. (Shifting a huge body around isn't easy!) They spend up to 86 percent of their day underwater. Often the only parts to be seen above water are their eyes and nostrils. They even sleep underwater. A sleeping hippo rises to the

OWEN AND MZEE

On December 26, 2004, a tsunami (giant wave) destroyed many parts of Asia and eastern Africa. The wave swept a group of hippos, including a young male calf and his mother, into the Indian Ocean. Out of the whole group, only the calf made it to safety. Less than a year old, the calf was rescued by wildlife rangers, who named him Owen. Without his mother, they didn't give Owen much chance to survive. They put him in Haller Park in Mombasa, Kenya. Owen soon went in search of a new mother. He chose a 130-year-old giant male tortoise named Mzee ("old man" in Swahili).

The rangers were amazed. The two swam, ate, and slept together. Owen followed Mzee just like he would follow his birth mother. He was also very protective of Mzee. The old tortoise showed Owen how to eat plants and where to sleep. In 2007, the park rangers brought Owen a hippo companion named Cleo. She wasn't as gentle with Mzee. The rangers moved the tortoise to another area of the park.

surface every few minutes, breathes out, takes another breath, and then sinks again. This action is not something a hippo needs to think about. It's as automatic as blinking is to humans.

Slow-moving or still, shallow waters are favorite napping areas for common hippos. In these places, they can stand on the bottom rather than having to swim. Calves find this easier too. They don't have to swim and nurse at the same time. Hippos avoid swift currents and places with big waves. The animals are likely to be pushed off their feet and swept away.

Whenever possible, hippos stay close to water. This gives them a place to hide when they are frightened. Pygmy hippos reach the water through the winding paths they have made through the thick forest. They also hide in the forest's low shrubs.

SWIMMING HIPPOS

Despite the amount of time hippos spend in the water, they are not very graceful swimmers. Still, their clumsy strokes move them faster than a person can swim or paddle a boat. Years ago, people didn't know how hippos managed to move so quickly underwater. Daring photographers gave the answer by filming hippos beneath the water. This is a dangerous task. A hippo may attack if it thinks the photographer is threatening it.

When a hippo moves through deep water, it pushes off the bottom with its hind legs and heads toward the surface. The hippo tucks its back legs up close to its body. This helps its balloon shape glide more easily through the water.

A hippo's bite is strong enough to kill a person. An attacking hippo can make holes in a boat with its tusks and can crush a boat with its body.

When it sinks back to the bottom, the hippo lands first on its front legs. After all four legs are down, the hippo is ready to push off again. Biologists call this kind of swimming **punting**. Although a punting hippo looks clumsy on land, it looks as if it were dancing on tiptoes on the river bottom. Punting helps the animal reach speeds of up to 20 miles per hour (32 km/h)!

This pygmy hippo is pushing off the bottom of the river as he swims, giving the hippo more speed.

35

Most of these common hippos have almost disappeared as they wallow in the mud.

Hippos don't rest in water because they're lazy. Unlike humans, they have no sweat glands. Hanging out in the water is an easy way to keep their skin cool and moist. Like the heat, insects are a constant irritation. Fortunately, hippos and mud are seldom far apart. When a hippo **wallows**, or rolls around in the mud, a muddy shield is left on the skin. The mud stops bugs from biting.

HELPING ONE ANOTHER

While lounging in the water, hippos provide a service to the community of plants and animals that live there. A hippo's feces are a source of food for algae and other tiny plants. In turn, fish nibble on the plants, and other animals eat the fish. A hippo's feet also stir up the mud on the bottom of the river or lake. The bottom-dwelling creatures tossed up with the mud are tasty meals for fish and other creatures. Catfish and sucker fish do hippos a favor in return. They clean the hippo's skin by eating algae and other materials that have collected on it. Hippos also open their mouths wide and let the fish swim in and pick food from around their molars.

A hippo also has bird friends to help keep its skin clean. The oxpecker picks off ticks and other parasites that dine on the hippo's blood. Cattle egrets, geese, and other waterbirds often sit on the backs of hippos as they rest in the water. These guests eat the insects they find around the hippos.

LET'S EAT!

About 2 hours before sunset, common hippos start moving around. This is their most active time. Most of their sounds occur in this part of the day. Calves do most of their playing. Mating takes place.

These birds find a meal on this common hippo napping in the water.

A common hippo munches on grass at a national park in Swaziland.

As twilight arrives, the hippos lumber out of the water. They trudge up the riverbank and through the grass to their feeding areas. Over time, they wear deep ruts in the ground. Within a mile (2 km) or so of the watering hole, each hippo branches off onto a path that leads to its own private feeding area. Scattered feces from earlier feeding trips help the hippo know it's on the right trail.

Hippos in the wild pluck grass, their favorite food, with their lips. Like walking lawn mowers, they waddle along. They move their heads from side to side and tear off mouthfuls of grass. The grassy areas where hippos graze are closely cut, as if they have been mown.

Hippos also eat tender shoots and leaves and fruit that has fallen from trees. Zoo hippos are fed about 100 pounds (45 kg) of vegetables, hay, and grains each day.

Except for cows that have calves with them, hippos usually graze alone. They spend most of the night grazing. They may wander from 3 to 6 miles (5–10 km) within their feeding areas. Dawn's light signals to hippos that they need to head back to the daytime safety of their wallowing areas.

Zoologists have watched common hippos in the wild. They report that herds tend to stay in the same area as long as water levels are about the same. When water levels drop, hippos seek new homes.

Hippos swim to the shore as twilight approaches. Hippos like to feed at night.

HIPPOS AND PEOPLE

PREDATORS MAY ATTACK CALVES AND SICK OR OLD ADULT hippos. But generally a hippo's worst enemies are people. Throughout history, humans have hunted hippos for their meat and for sport. The walls of many Egyptian tombs have drawings of people hunting hippos *(above)*. At one time, thousands of hippos lived along Egypt's Nile River. However, Europeans who visited or settled in Egypt in the 1700s and 1800s were eager hippo hunters. As a result, Egypt no longer has any wild hippos.

A TENSE RELATIONSHIP

Hippos play their own part in their violent relationship with humans. They kill about three hundred people each year. Many of these deaths could be avoided, if people—especially boaters—watched out for hippos. Rangers warn people never to get between a cow and her young or between any hippo and the water. But even in situations in which hippos are the attackers, they may still end up the losers. Humans who have survived a hippo attack have been known to strike back and kill their attacker.

During the past one hundred years, people have been using more of Africa's land for farming. Wet places where common hippos naturally live are also good for growing rice. Grazing hippos often invade rice paddies, destroying the farmer's crop and source of income. The forests of Liberia, the pygmy hippo's natural habitat, are being cut for farmland and wood. Although some pygmy hippos are in zoos, those in the wild could face extinction if their habitat is not protected. In particular, areas need to be set aside where hippos can roam freely and safely.

THANKS, DAD

In 1926, Harvey Firestone of the Firestone Tire and Rubber Company opened a huge rubber tree plantation in Liberia. (The rubber tree's sap, called latex, is made into tires and other rubber products.) In 1927, Harvey gave U.S. president Calvin Coolidge a male pygmy hippo from Liberia. Named Billy, the hippo eventually was sent to the National Zoo in Washington, D.C. He became the ancestor of most of the pygmy hippos living in U.S. zoos.

Below: The wet places where hippos like to live are also places where farmers try to grow rice.

IVORY HUNTERS

The newest threat to hippos is **poachers**, or illegal hunters. They kill the animals for their teeth. The hard, white substance that forms hippo and elephant tusks is called **ivory**. Throughout history, people have carved ivory into decorative objects such as jewelry, umbrella handles, and sculptures. Dentists used to make false teeth out of hippo ivory because it does not turn yellow.

Elephants were hunted for their ivory until they nearly became extinct. A worldwide ban on buying and selling elephant ivory started in 1989. It discouraged some poachers from killing them. Yet a steady demand for ivory trinkets makes poachers want to continue to get ivory. More of them have turned to hippos for their livelihood. Unfortunately, a large herd of wallowing hippos is an easy target for a poacher with a gun.

The declining numbers of both pygmy and common hippos have caught the attention of conservationists (people who want to protect wildlife). The Convention on International Trade in Endangered Species (CITES) has banned trade in pygmy hippos or any products made from them. So far, trade in common hippos is not banned. But international laws limit trade as a way to keep the population stable. These are only the first steps toward saving hippos. Educating people about these animals and the way they live is another. If the number of common hippos continues to drop, a ban on trading the ivory of common hippos may be necessary to save the species.

A man displays a hippo tusk *(left)*. Poachers kill hippos for their ivory tusks. This has reduced the hippo population in the wild.

Common hippos, like this group at a national park in Tanzania, need to be protected in order to survive.

Watching hippos in zoos can be fun and interesting. But those in the wild play an important role in the ecosystems, or communities of plants and animals, to which they belong. If hippos, like elephants, are hunted close to extinction, these ecosystems will be affected in ways we can't predict. All of us have a role in making sure these large and fascinating animals survive.

GLOSSARY

bulls: adult male hippos

calf: a baby hippo

canine teeth: large, sharp tusks in the front of a hippo's mouth that are used for fighting

cows: adult female hippos

crèche: the protected area near the water's edge where common hippo calves and their mothers live

dominant: the strongest male in an area

endangered: at risk of losing all members of a species forever

estrus: the period during which a female hippo is able to become pregnant

extinction: the death of all members of a species

feces: solid waste matter, or poop

fossil: plant or animal remains or other traces that have been preserved in stone

habitat: a plant or animal's natural living space

herbivores: animals that eat only plants

herd: a group of adult and young common hippos that live together in the same area

incisors: sharp front teeth that are used for fighting

ivory: a hard, white substance that forms the tusks (canines) of hippos and elephants

larynx: the part of the throat that is used to make sounds

molars: large, ridged back teeth that are used for grinding food

poachers: people who illegally hunt animals

predators: animals that hunt other animals for food

premolars: side teeth, between the canines and the molars, that are used for grinding food

punting: moving through the water by pushing off the bottom while tucking in the legs

species: a specific kind of plant or animal

territory: the area a bull claims and defends as his own for mating purposes

vulnerable: having low enough numbers that a plant or animal might completely die out if conservation efforts aren't made

wallows: rolls about or rests in damp, muddy places

SELECTED BIBLIOGRAPHY

Estes, Richard D. *The Safari Companion: A Guide to Watching African Mammals*. Rev. ed. White River Junction, VT: Chelsea Green Publishing Company, 1999.

Graves, Eleanor, ed. *Elephants and Other Land Giants*. New York: Time-Life Films, 1977.

Grzimek, Bernhard, Neil Schlager, and Donna Olendorf. *Grzimek's Animal Life Encyclopedia*. 2nd ed. Farmington Hills, MI: Gale, 2003.

IUCN. *Hippo Specialist Group of the World Conservation Union*. N.d. http://moray.ml.duke.edu/projects/hippos/ (June 26, 2007).

Lavine, Sigmund A. *Wonders of Hippos*. New York: Dodd, Mead Wonders Books, 1983.

Oliver, William L. R., ed. *Pigs, Peccaries and Hippos*. Gland, Switzerland: World Conservation Union, 1993.

PBS. "Hippo Beach." *Nature*. VHS South Burlington, VT: WNET, 2003.

WEBSITES

African Wildlife Foundation
http://www.awf.org
Visit the African Wildlife Foundation website and find out how to help protect Africa's endangered species.

Hippo World
http://members.aol.com/HippoPage/index.htm
Meet Horace the hippo and learn more about hippos with pictures, stories, and poems.

National Geographic Kids Magazine—Hippopotamus
http://www.nationalgeographic.com/kids/creature_feature/0009/hippos2.html
This site contains a lot of fun facts about hippos. It also includes maps, videos, and postcards.

Owen and Mzee
http://www.owenandmzee.com
This website is in honor of the unusual bond that developed between Owen, a common hippo calf, and Mzee, a very old tortoise. The site includes a kids' section with games, photos, and more.

FURTHER READING

Allen, Christina M. *Hippos in the Night: Autobiographical Adventures in Africa*. New York: HarperCollins, 2003.

Arnold, Caroline. *African Animals*. New York: HarperCollins, 1997.

Feldhake, Glenn. *Hippos: Natural History & Conservation*. Stillwater, MN: Voyageur Press, 2005.

Hatkoff, Isabell, Craig Hatkoff, and Paula Kahumbu. *Owen & Mzee: The Language of Friendship*. New York: Scholastic, 2007.

————. *Owen & Mzee: The True Story of a Remarkable Friendship*. New York: Scholastic, 2006.

Melnicove, Mark, and Margy Burns Knight. *Africa Is Not a Country*. Minneapolis: Millbrook Press, 2002.

Walker, Sally M. *Rhinos*. Minneapolis: Lerner Publications Company, 2007.

INDEX

ABOUT THE AUTHOR

Sally M. Walker is the author of many award-winning nonfiction books for young readers. She wrote *Secrets of a Civil War Submarine: Solving the Mysteries of the H. L. Hunley*, which won the prestigious Sibert award in 2006. When she isn't busy writing or doing research for books, Walker works as a children's literature consultant. She gives presentations at many reading conferences and has taught at Northern Illinois University.

PHOTO ACKNOWLEDGEMENTS

The images in this book are used with permission of: © Photodisc/Getty Images, all backgrounds on pp. 1, 5, 6, 9, 10, 13, 17, 18, 20, 21, 22, 23, 25, 26, 33, 34, 35, 40, 41, 44, 45, 46, 47, 48; © Gerry Ellis/Science Faction/Getty Images, pp. 2–3; © age fotostock/SuperStock, pp. 4, 10, 14, 15 (top), 16 (top), 17, 28 (bottom), 38, 41; © iStockphoto.com/ Nico Smit, p. 5; © Brandon Cole/Visuals Unlimited, p. 6; © Photodisc/Getty Images, pp. 7, 15 (bottom); © Laura Westlund/Independent Picture Service, pp. 8, 11 (bottom); © Patricio Robles Gil/Sierra Madre/Minden Pictures, p. 9; © Steve Vates/Alamy, p. 11 (top); © Dani/Jeske/Animals Animals, p. 12 (top); © Tom & Pat Leeson, p. 12 (bottom); © Cliff Keeler/Alamy, p. 13; © Dennis Nigel/Bios/Peter Arnold, Inc., p. 16 (bottom); © James P. Rowan, pp. 18, 31 (top), 33, 37; © Royalty-Free/CORBIS, p. 19; © Holger Ehlers/Alamy, p. 20; © Panoramic Images/Getty Images, p. 21; © Andrew Parkinson/naturepl.com, p. 22; © Danita Delimont/Alamy, p. 23; © Steve Bloom Images/Alamy, p. 24; © Anup Shah/Stone/Getty Images, p. 25; Courtesy of the Louisville Zoo, Kara Bussabarger, photographer, p. 26; © Georgette Douwma/naturepl.com, p. 27; © iStockphoto.com/Peter Miller, p. 28 (top); © AfriPics.com/Alamy, p. 29; © Suzi Eszterhas/Minden Pictures/Getty Images, p. 30; © Ariadne Van Zandbergen/Alamy, p. 31 (bottom); © Andrew Fox/Alamy, p. 32; © Peter Greste/AFP/Getty Images, p. 34; © Anup Shah/naturepl.com, p. 35; © iStockphoto.com/ Vera Bogaerts, p. 36; © Gerry Ellis/Minden Pictures, p. 39; © Werner Forman/Art Resource, NY, p. 40; © J. Short/ Art Directors, p. 42; © iStockphoto.com/Joe McDaniel, p. 43; © iStockphoto.com/Hansjoerg Richter, p. 46.

Front cover: © Digital Vision/Getty Images.
Back cover: © Photodisc/Getty Images.